Steck Vaughn

Social Studies

Level B

People AND Places Nearby

PROGRAM CONSULTANTS

Sonya Abbye Taylor, Senior Associate
Professional Development Network, Inc.
(Education Consultant)
New Rochelle, N.Y.
and
Field Supervisor and Instructor
Manhattanville College
Purchase, N.Y.

Barbara C. Donahue, Principal
Burlington County Special Services School District
Westampton, N.J.

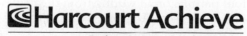

Harcourt Achieve

Rigby • Saxon • Steck-Vaughn

www.HarcourtAchieve.com
1.800.531.5015

ACKNOWLEDGMENTS

Photo Credits: P.5 ©Michael Newman/PhotoEdit; p.10 (bottom left) ©Jonathon Rawle/Stock Boston, (bottom right) Catherine Wessel/CORBIS; p.11 (bottom left) ©Eddie Rodriguez, (bottom right) ©George Roose/Peter Arnold; p.12 (bottom left) ©Owen Franken/Stock Boston, (bottom right) ©John Dago/Getty Images; p.18 ©National Portrait Gallery, Smithsonian Institution/Art Resource, NY; p.21 ©Michael Newman/PhotoEdit; p.22 ©W. Cody/CORBIS; p.23 ©John Cancalosi/Peter Arnold; p.34 ©National Portrait Gallery, Smithsonian Institution/Art Resource, NY; p.37 ©W. Cody/CORBIS; p.38 ©Superstock; p.41 ©Superstock; p.42 (left) ©Joan Menschenfreund, (right) ©Michal Heron; p.43 (left) ©Stewart Cohen/Getty Images, (right) ©Robert Brenner/PhotoEdit; p.44 ©David Barnes/Photo Researchers; p.45 ©Jean Hosking/CORBIS; p.48 (right and bottom left) ©Joan Menschenfreund; p.49 (top) ©Olivier Rebbot/Stock Boston, (bottom) ©Eddie Rodriguez; p.53 (bottom left) ©Tom McCarthy/Unicorn Stock Photos, (bottom right) ©Jeff Greenberg/Unicorn Stock Photos; p.54 ©Arthur Tilley/Getty Images; p.55 ©Abe Rezny/The Image Works; p.56 ©Eddie Rodriguez; p.58 George Hall/Woodfin Camp and Associates; p.59 ©U.S. Treasury Department, Bureau of Printing and Engraving; p.62 ©Superstock; p.63 ©Richard Hutchings/PhotoEdit; p.64 ©Richard Hutchings; p.66 (all) ©Alfonso Barrios; p.68 (left, right) ©Joan Menschenfreund, (middle) ©Quinn Stewart; p.74 ©Keith Jewell; p.75 (top right) ©National Portrait Gallery, Smithsonian Institution/Art Resource, NY, (bottom) ©The Collection of the New-York Historical Society; p.81 ©John Mead/ Science Photo Library/Photo Researchers; p.85 ©Richard Hutchings/PhotoEdit; p.86 ©Bachmann/The Image Works; pp.87, 88 ©Eddie Rodriguez; p.89 (top) ©Diana Bourdez, (bottom) ©Joan Menschenfreund; p.90 ©Michal Heron; p.91 (top left) ©Richard Hutchings, (top right) ©Donald Dietz/Stock Boston, (bottom) ©Joan Menschenfreund; p.92 ©Bob Daemmrich/The Image Works; p.95 (left) ©David Frazier/Photo Researchers, (right) Allan A. Philiba; p.96 ©Eddie Rodriguez; p.97 (top) ©John Henley/CORBIS, (middle) ©Superstock; p.98 ©Hulleah Tsinhnahjinnie/©1990 courtesy Steinbaum Krauss Gallery, NCY; p.99 (bottom left) ©Marvin Newman/Woodfin Camp & Associates, (bottom right) ©Karen Su/CORBIS; p.102 ©Bachmann/The Image Works.

Additional photography by Getty Royalty Free and Royalty-Free CORBIS.

ISBN: 0-7398-9219-3

3 4 5 6 7 8 9 030 10 09 08 07 06

Contents

Neighborhoods Today

People live together in many different ways.
You live with your family.

- Who lives next door?

- What is the place like where you live?

UNIT PROJECT

Work with some classmates. Look at your neighborhood. What is your neighborhood like? Think of some places in your neighborhood. Write words that describe them. Draw pictures. Make a book about your neighborhood.

Neighborhoods Are for Living

The people who live near you are your **neighbors.** You are their neighbor. A **neighborhood** is a place where people live, work, and play.

This is a picture of Jenny's neighborhood.

 Circle the places in Jenny's neighborhood that you have in your neighborhood.

Find one thing neighbors are doing together. Write your answer here.

_____

- -

_____

Jenny is going to draw a **map** of her neighborhood. A map is a drawing of a place. It shows whether things are near or far apart. A map can also show what is to the left or right of something else.

Jenny is making a **map key.** The map key shows what the pictures on the map mean.

Here is part of Jenny's map key.

 Put a ✔ next to the picture of the house.

What does the picture with the book stand for? Write your answer here.

_____

_ _ _ _ _ _ _ _ _ _ _ _ _ _ _ _ _ _

_____

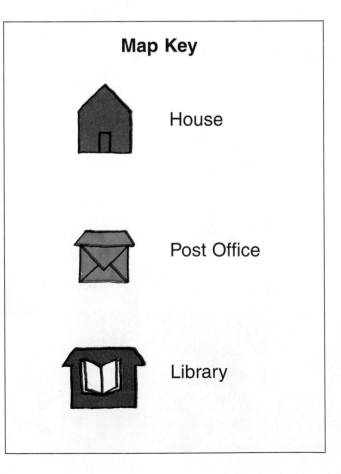

Map Key

House

Post Office

Library

This is Jenny's map of her neighborhood.

 Circle the places where people live.

Put a ✔ next to a place that is near the Art Museum.

A **compass rose** shows you which ways are north, south, east, and west. These ways are called **directions.** Find the compass rose.

 What is north of the library? Draw a line under it.

Jenny's Neighborhood

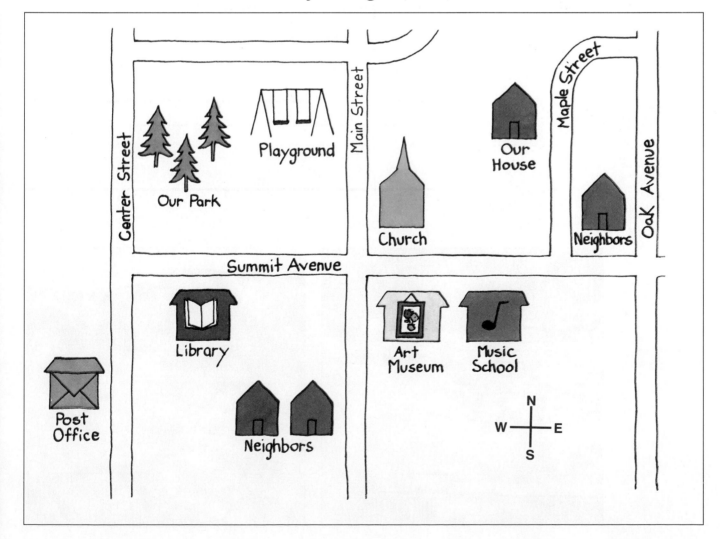

9

Mountain

Ocean

Neighborhoods are found in many different places. Some neighborhoods are in the **mountains.** A mountain is land that is very high. It is cold high up in the mountains. Sometimes there is snow at the top. People often ski in mountain neighborhoods.

Some neighborhoods are near **oceans.** An ocean is a large body of salt water. People may own boats and work to catch fish in ocean neighborhoods.

 Look at the pictures. Put an X above the picture of a neighborhood in the mountains.

What kinds of clothes would you wear if you lived high in the mountains? Why?

_____

— — — — — — — — — — — — — — — —

_____

_____

— — — — — — — — — — — — — — — —

_____

Other neighborhoods are found on flat lands called **plains.** Many farms are found on the plains. This is because it is easier to farm on flat land than on hilly land.

You will also find neighborhoods near **rivers.** A river is a long stream of water that flows across land. Some rivers are so large that big ships can go on them.

Plain

River

🌐 **Look at the pictures below. Circle the place you would like to visit.**

Where is your neighborhood? Is it near mountains? Is it near the ocean? Is there a river nearby?

Around The Globe

Where People Live

People live in neighborhoods all around the world. These neighborhoods may be near oceans. Or they may be in the mountains. One thing is the same about all of them. All neighborhoods have places for people to live, work, and play.

Look at these pictures. They show neighborhoods in countries far away. Picture 1 shows a neighborhood in Nigeria. Picture 2 shows a neighborhood in Thailand.

 How are these neighborhoods alike? Write your answer here.

_____

_ _

_____

_ _

_____

CHAPTER ✓ CHECKUP

Use the words in the Word Box to finish each sentence. Write the words on the lines.

Word Box

compass rose
mountains
map key
plains

1. Farms are found on flat lands called

_____

_ _ _ _ _ _ _ _ _ _ _ _ _ _ _ _ _ _

_____ .

2. Some neighborhoods are on very high land called

_____

_ _

_____ .

3. You can find directions on a map by using the

_____

_ _

_____ .

4. You can learn about the pictures on a map in the

_____

_ _

_____ .

THINKING AND WRITING Look at Picture 2 on page 12. Tell one way your neighborhood is like this neighborhood in Thailand. Tell one way it is different. Write your answers here.

_____

_ _

Like _____

_____

_ _

Different _____

Neighborhoods Change

The picture shows what one neighborhood looked like 100 years ago. Not many people lived there. There were no cars. People rode in carts pulled by horses. Or they rode on the horses.

 Look at the picture. Draw a line below the things you would not see in a neighborhood today.

This picture shows the same neighborhood today. **Inventions** have changed how people get from place to place and where people live. Inventions are things made for the first time.

 Look at both pictures. What is one way inventions have changed the neighborhood? Circle something new shown in the picture here.

_____

- -

_____

- -

Neighborhoods can change in many ways. People move into the neighborhood or move away. Houses are fixed and painted.

Look at the picture of this house.

■ Put an **X** on things that need to be fixed.

Circle what you would fix first.

The family fixed the old house.

Write a <u>C</u> on all the things they changed.

Have places in your neighborhood changed?
Which places are new? Which are being fixed?
Make a list of places. Draw pictures of the places.

What would your neighborhood be like without any lights? It would be dark. It would not be easy to read or to see where you are going. Thomas Edison made the first light bulb. These light bulbs changed the way neighborhoods looked at night.

Edison liked to think of new ways of doing things. He spent his life making inventions. He also thought of ways to make old things better. The telephone is one thing he made work better.

You use lights every day. Could you do the same things without lights? List things you could not do.

_____

_ _ _ _ _ _ _ _ _ _ _ _ _ _ _ _ _ _ _

_____

Read each sentence. Write **T** on the line if the sentence is true. Write **F** if it is false.

—————

— — — — **1.** Long ago people used carts pulled by horses to get
—————   around.

— — — — **2.** When no one takes care of a neighborhood, it looks
—————   beautiful.

— — — — **3.** People can paint and fix the houses in a neighborhood.
—————

— — — — **4.** Inventions can change neighborhoods.
—————

— — — — **5.** All neighborhoods look the same.
—————

 What are two ways neighborhoods change? Write your answers here.

— —
———

— —
———

Unit 1 Skill Builder

Using a Map

Look at the map and the map key. Read each sentence. Do what it tells you.

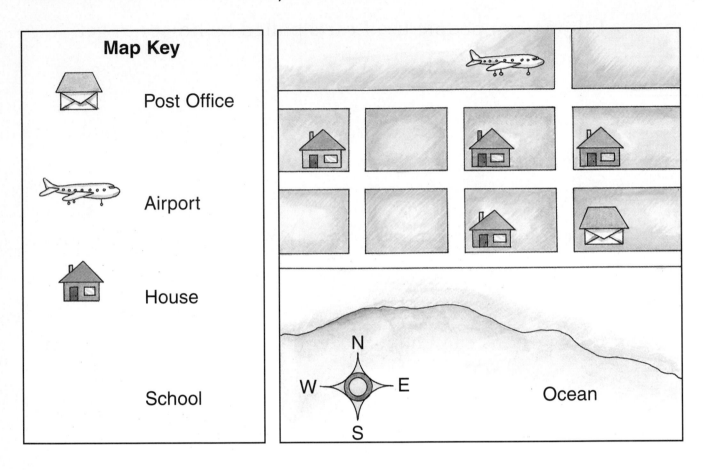

1. Put an <u>A</u> over the airport.

2. Draw a circle around the house west of the post office.

3. Draw a picture for a school. Put it in the map key. Then, draw it on the map.

4. How can you get from the airport to the post office? Draw a line on the map to show how to get from the airport to the post office.

Talk with your classmates about your neighborhood. Answer these questions.

- **What is your neighborhood like?**

- **What are some of the places in your neighborhood?**

- **What rivers, ocean, or mountains are near your neighborhood?**

Now decide how you will present your project. Try one of these ideas or think of another one.

➤ Make your book. Use words and sentences to tell about your neighborhood. Use your pictures in your book.

➤ Draw a map of your neighborhood. Show streets and the places where people live, work, and play. Draw a compass rose. Draw a map key.

Neighborhoods Long Ago

Look at this picture. It shows how the United States must have looked long, long ago. There were no towns and cities. But there were people living here.

- Who were the first people to live in the United States long, long ago?

- How did they live?

UNIT PROJECT

Work with your classmates to learn about American Indians. Choose one group. You might choose a group that lived in your area long ago. Find out about them.

The First Americans

American Indians were the first people to live in our country. American Indians lived together in groups. Some groups were large. Others had only a few families. These groups lived in different parts of the country.

American Indians lived in many kinds of houses. They built their houses from things they found where they lived. The picture shows the way one group lived. These houses were built of rock and clay. They were built on a narrow cliff.

How are these American Indian homes like homes in a neighborhood? Write your answer here.

_____

_____

_____

23

Some American Indian groups lived on the plains. These American Indians were hunters. They used spears and bows and arrows to hunt **buffalo.** Buffalo are large animals that lived on the plains.

American Indians used all parts of the buffalo. They ate the buffalo meat. They used the bones for tools. They used the hide, or skin, for clothing and shoes. They also used the hide to cover their houses. These houses were called tepees.

Circle three things in the picture that could have been made from buffalo hide.

UNIT PROJECT Tip Learn about the animals that live in your area. How were animals useful to the American Indian group you chose?

American Indians had to find or grow all their food. Everyone helped in getting the food. American Indians living on the plains hunted buffalo in the summer. The men did the hunting. They had to get enough buffalo meat to last all winter. After the hunt the women cooked or dried the meat. They dried it to make it last through the winter.

Other groups of American Indians were farmers. They planted corn and beans. These American Indians made their own tools for farming. They used stone, wood, and clay to make their tools.

What would you like to ask an American Indian who lived long ago? Write your question here.

_____

_____

_____

What have you learned about American Indians and how they lived? The **chart** below will help you remember. A chart puts facts in order.

American Indians Long Ago	
Homes	built or made homes
Food	hunted, fished, or grew food
Clothing	made all clothes

 Find the word *Homes* on the chart. The box next to it tells more about homes. How did the American Indians of long ago get their homes? Write your answer here.

_____

_____

_____

_____

Find the word *Clothing* on the chart. How did the American Indians get their clothing? Write your answer here.

_____

_____

_____

_____

26

The Aztecs

You have read about American Indians who lived in the United States. American Indians also lived in other parts of the Americas. The Aztecs were American Indians who lived in Mexico.

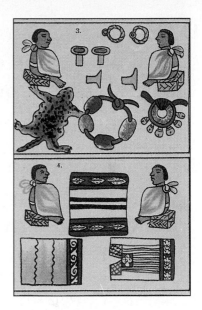

The Aztecs wrote with pictures instead of letters. Each picture told an idea or part of an idea. The Aztecs used these pictures to write about important things that happened.

You can write a story using pictures. Think about what you want to say. Use a picture instead of a word. Here is one to read.

We wanted to go to the ⬯ .

But a 🌲 fell down. It blocked the ⟍⟍ .

■ **Write a story using pictures. Write your story here.**

_____

_ _

_____

_ _

_____

CHAPTER ✓ CHECKUP

Finish each sentence. Circle the correct words.

1. American Indians
   lived only by the ocean.
   were all part of one group.
   were the first Americans.

2. American Indians got their food by
   going to the store.
   hunting and farming.
   going to a restaurant.

3. Some American Indians used buffalo hide to make
   paper.
   clothing.
   juice.

4. The Aztecs
   were not American Indians.
   lived in the United States.
   wrote with pictures instead of letters.

THINKING AND WRITING American Indians of long ago built houses from the things they found where they lived. What could American Indians who lived in your area have used for houses?

_____

‒ ‒

_____

CHAPTER 4

Neighborhoods of Early America

American Indians had lived here for many, many years. Then, in 1492, Christopher Columbus came here from Spain. Spain is a country in Europe. Columbus was looking for a new way to reach other land. He sailed west across the Atlantic Ocean. He landed on a small island near the United States.

Look at the map of the world below. The blue parts show water. The other parts are land. The dotted line shows where Columbus sailed.

Find the Atlantic Ocean. Draw an <u>X</u> on it.

Trace the way that Columbus sailed to America.

Each large area of land is called a continent. There are seven continents. Draw a <u>C</u> on the continent of North America.

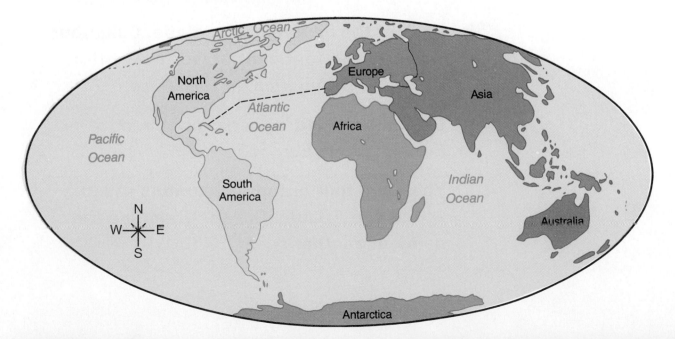

You can also find where Columbus sailed on a **globe.** A globe is a model of Earth. It is round like a ball. You can see only one half of it at one time.

The picture shows each half of the globe. The key tells you that the blue parts of the globe show water. The green parts show land.

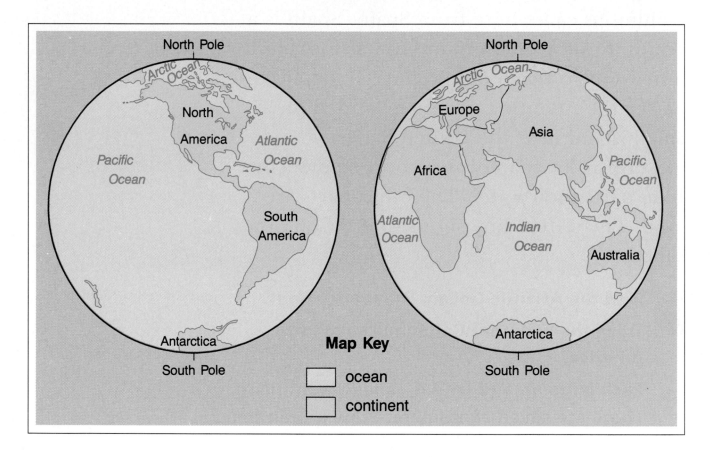

 Look at the picture of the globe. Columbus sailed to the continent of North America. Circle North America on the globe.

Columbus sailed from the continent of Europe. Circle Europe.

There are four oceans. Columbus sailed across the Atlantic Ocean. Underline the name of another ocean.

Many groups of people sailed across the Atlantic Ocean after Columbus. One group was the Pilgrims. They came from England. England is a country in Europe. The Pilgrims built a new town. They called it Plymouth.

The Pilgrims' first winter in America was long and cold. Many of the Pilgrims died. In the spring they had to learn to plant and grow food. Their neighbors were American Indians. The American Indians showed the Pilgrims how to hunt, fish, and plant corn.

What could you do to help someone who moved to your neighborhood? Write your answer here.

_____

_ _

_____

The Pilgrims wanted to thank their American Indian neighbors for their help. The Pilgrims and American Indians sat down and ate together. This was the very first Thanksgiving dinner. Today we still eat Thanksgiving dinner with our family, friends, and neighbors.

Tell one way the Pilgrims and American Indians were good neighbors. Write your answer here.

_____

_ _ _ _ _ _ _ _ _ _ _ _ _ _ _ _ _ _

_____

With your classmates, learn how American Indians got food. Did your group farm? Did they hunt? What tools did they use to get food?

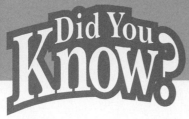

The first English town in America that lasted was Jamestown. The town grew slowly at first. The people found it hard to live in America. American Indians helped them learn. The English people cut down trees and built houses. They learned to hunt and fish and to plant corn and other crops. Then Jamestown grew and grew.

 Look at the picture of Jamestown. How is it like a neighborhood today? Write your answer here.

_____

_____

_____

Pocahontas was an American Indian who lived long ago. She helped the people of Jamestown and the American Indians become friends. Pocahontas learned to speak English. Then Pocahontas helped the English people learn how to live in their new land.

Ætatis suæ 21. Aº. 1616.

Matoaks als Rebecka daughter to the mighty Prince Powhatan Emperour of Attanoughkomouck als Virginia converted and baptized in the Christian faith, and Wife to the wor.ll Mr Tho. Rolff.

 A new student has come to your school. She cannot speak English. How can you tell her what she needs to know? Write your answer here.

_____

_ _ _ _ _ _ _ _ _ _ _ _ _ _ _ _ _ _

_____

_ _ _ _ _ _ _ _ _ _ _ _ _ _ _ _ _ _

_____

CHAPTER CHECKUP

Use the words in the Word Box to finish each sentence. Write the words on the lines.

Word Box

Atlantic
Earth
Thanksgiving
continent

1. A globe is a model of

_____

- - - - - - - - - - - - - - - - - - - -

_____ .

2. A very large area of land is called a

_____

- -

_____ .

3. Columbus sailed across the

_____

- -

_____ Ocean.

4. The Pilgrims and the American Indians ate together on the first

_____

- -

_____ .

THINKING AND WRITING How were the people who built Plymouth and Jamestown alike? Tell one way. Write your answer here.

_____

- -

_____

- -

_____

Unit 2 Skill Builder
Reading a World Map

You remember that a world map is a picture of Earth. Look at the world map and the compass rose. Read each sentence. Do what it tells you.

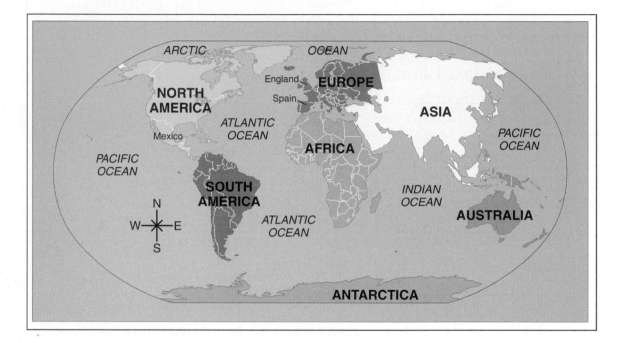

1. The Pilgrims sailed from England to North America. What ocean did they cross?

   _____

   _ _ _ _ _ _ _ _ _ _ _ _ _ _ _ _ _

   _____

2. The Aztecs lived in Mexico. Put an <u>X</u> on Mexico.

3. Columbus sailed from Spain. Put a <u>C</u> on the continent Spain is a part of.

Work with your classmates. Talk about answers to questions like these.

- **Which groups of American Indians lived in your area?**

- **What animals lived in your area?**

- **In the past how did the American Indians in your area get food?**

Now decide how you will present your project. Try one of these ideas or think of another one.

➤ Make a museum about the American Indian group that you chose. A museum is a place that shows important things. Put things in your museum. What will you put in your museum?

➤ Build a model of houses like those used by an American Indian group in your area. Use clay, paper, and other things.

➤ Draw pictures showing how this American Indian group lived. Show the clothing they wore. Show how they hunted, fished, or farmed.

People Work in Many Places

Your neighbors work in many different jobs. They may work in your neighborhood or in other neighborhoods.

- Why do people have jobs?

- What kinds of jobs do they have?

- How do their jobs help you?

UNIT PROJECT

Start a team project. Work with a group of classmates. Find out about different kinds of workers. Ask your teacher, librarian, and other adults about jobs people do. Talk to workers you meet. List jobs people do. Work on your project as you read Unit 3.

People Give Us Goods and Services

Needs are things people must have to live. Food, clothes, and a place to live are three needs that all people have.

Wants are things people would like to have. Toys, trips, and pets are some of the things people want.

The children in one class want different things. Look at the picture graph. A **picture graph** uses pictures to show facts. This picture graph shows how many children want each thing.

Five children want a ball. Color the 5 balls on the graph.

Three children want a kite. Draw 3 kites on line 2.

One child wants a hat. Draw 1 hat on line 3.

What we want	How many?
1 ball	◯ ◯ ◯ ◯ ◯
2 kite	
3 hat	

Many people work in your **community.** A community is a town or city where people live, work, and play. There are many neighborhoods in one community. Your neighbors work to make the things you need and want. These things are called **goods.**

Goods are made in a factory. These pictures show a toy factory. The toys are goods.

People have different jobs in a factory. Look at the pictures. These people work with machines. The machines help the workers do their jobs. What does each worker do?

Which worker makes a part for the toy? Put a <u>P</u> over the picture.

Which worker puts the toys in boxes? Put a <u>B</u> over the picture.

40

Sometimes many people work together to make goods. Look at the picture below. An automobile is so big that it takes many people to make it. Each person does a different job.

Sometimes people make different parts of a good. Then the parts are sent to one place to be put together. The space shuttle is made this way.

People often use machines to make goods. The machines make the work easier. Machines also help workers do their jobs faster.

 Look at the picture. What machines are the workers using to make the cars? Circle the machines.

Some people in the community work to help us. They give us **services.** A service is a job someone does to help other people. People who work in services do not make goods.

Your community has workers who give services. There are workers who keep the neighborhoods clean. Firefighters put out fires. Police officers work to keep your neighborhood safe. Doctors and nurses care for people who are sick. Your community has these services to help make your neighborhood better.

Look at the pictures. They show some community workers. What do these people do? Write your answer under each picture.

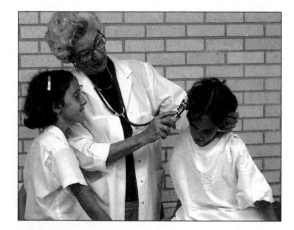

1. _____

2. _____

Many businesses give services too. People work together at service businesses to help others. A restaurant is a service business. People there cook and serve food. A television station is also a service business. The news is one service a television station gives. Many people work together to bring news to people all over the United States.

What workers have given you a service? Write the names of two jobs here.

———————————————————————————

1. ———————————————————————————

2. ———————————————————————————

PROJECT Tip What kinds of jobs do adults you know have? Ask them what they do at their jobs. Do most of the jobs give services or make goods? List the jobs.

How We Get Goods

How do goods get to the people who need them? Many things we need or want are made far from where we live.

Many goods may be sent from place to place on trains and trucks. Some goods, like milk, must be kept cold. Milk is moved in a special kind of truck.

There are special train cars to move goods, too. There are train cars for moving heavy goods, like tractors. Other train cars are built to carry food, like corn.

 Do you think ice cream is moved in a special truck? Why? Write your answer here.

_____

_____

_____

_____

Goods from Far Away

Some goods we need and want come from other countries. We need people in other countries to make or grow these foods for us.

We do not grow all the food we eat in the United States. Some food is grown in other countries. For instance, some bananas we eat come from Brazil. Brazil is a country on the continent of South America.

Some of the rubber we use comes from Sri Lanka. Sri Lanka is in Asia. Rubber trees grow there. People work in rubber tree forests to get the rubber. It is made into many goods that we use.

 Do you use goods made of rubber? Does your family? Make a list. Write your list here.

_____

_____

_____

_____

_____

_____

_____

_____

Read each sentence. Find the word in the Word Box to finish each sentence. Write the word on the lines.

1. A town or city with many neighborhoods is a

_____

— — — — — — — — — — — — — — — — — — — —

_____ .

2. Food, clothes, and a place to live are

_____

— —

_____ .

3. The things people make to meet our needs and wants are

_____

— —

_____ .

4. The post office worker gives us a

_____

— —

_____ .

Look at the workers in the pictures. Do they give us goods, or do they give us services? Write your answer here.

_____

— — — — — — — — — — — — — — — — — — —

_____

— — — — — — — — — — — — — — — — — — —

_____

Firefighter

Police Officer

CHAPTER 6

Why People Work

How do people choose what kinds of jobs they have? Sometimes people do what they really like. Teachers like working with children and helping them learn. A baseball player really likes to play baseball. These people enjoy doing their jobs.

Think about what you like to do. What kind of job would you like? Write your answer here.

_____

_ _

_____

Draw a picture of yourself doing the job you like. Draw your picture in the box below.

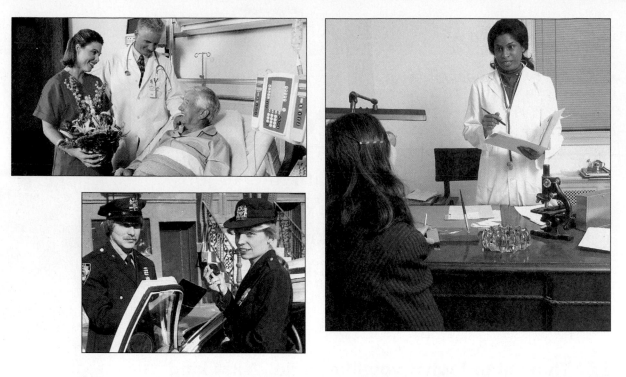

Some people choose a job because they want to help others. These people care for us when we are sick. They keep us safe. We need people to do these jobs.

Look around your school. What is one job that must be done every day? Who does it? Write your answer here.

_____

_____

_____

_____

_____

_____

UNIT PROJECT Tip

Work with your classmates. Think of jobs in your community. Ask some workers why they work. Why did they choose their jobs?

Sometimes people have special jobs because of where they live. Many people in the neighborhood may have the same kinds of jobs.

People living near water may fish or work on a boat. Other people have jobs fixing boats. Still other people sell things needed for fishing.

Think about other places that people live. What kinds of jobs do people have on the plains? What kinds of jobs do people have in the mountains?

 Look at picture 1. This worker lives and works near the water. Circle his job.

fixing boats

painting

unloading fish

 Look at picture 2. This worker lives in the mountains. There is a lot of snow in the mountains. Circle his job.

teaching

moving snow

farming

Who is working in the picture above? The teacher and the children are working. Think of all the jobs you do in school. Your most important job is to learn. But you have other jobs, too. Keeping your classroom clean is one job.

Look at the picture. Circle each person who is working.

What kinds of jobs are done at your home? Someone has to cook and clean. Someone has to wash the clothes. What kinds of jobs do you have at home?

Name one job you have at home. Write your answer here.

_____

- - - - - - - - - - - - - - - - - - - -

_____

Most people are paid to work. Sometimes people will work without pay. These people are **volunteers.** Volunteers choose to work for free. A **slave** is someone who is *forced* to work without pay. Slaves are not free. They cannot choose where to work or live. Long ago, some people in the United States were slaves.

Harriet Tubman was a woman who helped slaves escape to freedom. Harriet Tubman was born a slave in the state of Maryland. She escaped from slavery when she was 30 years old. Later she went back to Maryland. She wanted to help other slaves become free. She went back to Maryland 19 times. Each time she led more slaves to freedom. In all, she helped 300 slaves escape.

What job would you like to do to help people? Write your answer here.

_____

_____

_____

_____

_____

_____

Read each sentence. Write **T** on the line if the sentence is true.
Write **F** if it is false.

_____ **1.** No one likes to work.

_____ **2.** Some people choose a job because they want to help others.

_____ **3.** Some people have special jobs because of where they live.

_____ **4.** You have many jobs at school.

 Name a job you would like to do to make your neighborhood a better place to live. Tell why you want to do that job. Write your answer here.

_____

_____

_____

Where Does the Money Go?

The goods and services people need and want cost money. People must work to make money. The money people get for doing a job is called their **income.**

Most people do not have enough money to buy all they need and want. They must choose how to spend their income. They think about what they need and want most. Then they think about how much money they have.

How are these people spending their income? Draw an <u>N</u> on the person buying something that is a need.

Draw a <u>W</u> on the person buying something that is a want.

Many people use a **budget** to help them spend their money. A budget is a plan for how to spend money. A budget helps you know how much money you have and how much you can spend.

The García family wants to go on a trip. They are making a budget. Put an X next to each question about a budget that they must answer.

_____

_ _ _ _

_____ How much will the trip cost?

_____

_ _ _ _

_____ How much income do we have?

_____

_ _ _ _

_____ Where should we go?

_____

_ _ _ _

_____ What clothes shall we take?

When people make a budget, they list their needs first. Then they write down how much the goods and services they need will cost. Finally, they write down their income. The budget will show how much income will be left after paying for their needs.

Money that is left can be spent on goods and services people want. They cannot buy all they want. So they must choose those things they want the most.

Pretend that after buying your needs, you have $5.00 left to buy wants. Look at the list.

WANTS

Book $4.00	Crayons $2.00
Puzzle $3.00	Game $6.00
Ball $1.00	

Which wants can you buy? Write your answer here.

_____

_____

_____

_____

_____

UNIT PROJECT Tip

Remember that a volunteer is a person who chooses to work without pay. Think about your school and community. What kinds of volunteer jobs can children do? Ask about other kinds of volunteer jobs in your community. Make a list of volunteer jobs in your community.

Sometimes people want to buy things that cost a lot of money. They may want a car, a bicycle, or a television. People may save money to buy these things. They put money in a bank a little at a time. After a while, they have enough money to buy what they want. Money that is put in a safe place like a bank is called **savings.** Savings are an important part of a budget.

Do you have a piggy bank at home? Do you put money in it every week? If you do, then you have some savings, too.

What would you like to save money for? Draw a picture of it here.

Communities give services to the people who live in them. Police officers and other workers give these services. The communities must pay these workers. People give money to the community where they live. The money people pay to the community is called **taxes.**

 Look at the pictures. The community pays these people with tax money. How does each person help you? Write your answer next to the picture.

Teacher

Police Officer

Librarian

Communities need tax money for other things, too. Look at the picture above. It shows roads and bridges. Tax money is used to build roads and bridges like these. Taxes also pay to have the roads fixed.

Sometimes the community library needs new books. Tax money is used to buy the books. Taxes are used to build new schools or to fix up old ones. Taxes are used for all these things and more. Taxes help make your community a better place to live.

 Think about your community. What would happen if no one fixed a big hole in the street? Write your answer here.

_____

_____

_____

_____

Making Money

All our money is made in factories owned by the government. Coins are one kind of money. First, big sheets of metal are cut into circles. Then the circles are heated. The words and pictures are pressed into them.

Paper money is printed on large sheets of paper. Each sheet has 32 bills printed on it. The bills are then cut apart.

Coins and paper money show the dates they were made. They also have pictures of famous Americans on them. When new money is made, an artist makes a drawing. Then the picture is engraved, or carved, onto a steel plate.

Pretend the government is paying you to make a new bill. What would you show on it? Draw your new bill here.

Read each question. Circle the correct answer.

1. Why do people make budgets?

to help them choose services they want

to help them plan how to spend their money

to help them earn money

2. What is one reason we need savings?

to buy things we want that cost a lot of money

to buy food

to pay for community services

3. How do communities pay for the services they give people who live in them?

They use someone's income.

They do not pay for services.

They use the money they get from taxes.

THINKING AND WRITING What would happen if people did not pay taxes? Tell two things. Write your answer here.

_____

_____

_____

Unit 3 Skill Builder
Using a Picture Graph

The picture graph shows how many people give services to a community. Look at the picture graph. Then answer the questions.

Kinds of Service Workers	How many?
Judges	
School bus drivers	
City park workers	

1. How many judges work for the community?

   _____

   _

   _____

2. How many school bus drivers are there?

   _____

   _

   _____

3. The community also pays 6 city park workers. Draw a tree on the graph for each worker.

4. Name two things in your school that you could tell about on a picture graph.

   _

   _____

   _

   _____

Now it's time to finish your project. Think about what you learned about workers. Talk with your classmates. Answer these questions together.

- **What kinds of work do people you know do?**
- **What kinds of jobs do people in your community have?**
- **What can volunteer workers do?**
- **What kind of volunteer work can children do?**

Now decide how you will present your project. Try one of these ideas or think of another one.

➤ Work with your team to write a story about someone who has a job you learned about. Tell what the person does at work. Is the person a volunteer, a service worker, or does the person make goods?

➤ Draw some pictures of workers showing what each worker does. Show your pictures to other teams and tell them about the workers.

➤ Make a poster of jobs people do. Show on the poster if the workers are service workers, volunteers, or workers who make goods.

People Make Rules and Laws

People of all ages live, work, and play together in neighborhoods.

- How do people get along with each other?
- How do people work together to fix problems?

UNIT PROJECT

Start a team project. Think about your school. Work with your team to make a rule that would make your school better for everyone. Do this as you read Unit 4.

Rules and Laws for Everyone

People make **rules.** Rules tell us what to do or what not to do. They help us work and play together.

Rules are important. Some rules keep us safe. Other rules keep the places we live in or work in safe. Still other rules keep things fair.

These children are in their school library. What rules are they following? How do the rules help them work and play together?

 What is one rule you follow at school? Write your answer here.

_____

— — — — — — — — — — — — — — — — — — —

_____

Look at the pictures. They show rules you may have in your neighborhood. What rules do these pictures tell about?

Draw a line from the rule to the correct picture.

Each player gets a turn at bat.

Wait your turn in line without fooling around.

Circle the child who is not following the rule.

Why is it important for everyone to follow this rule? Write your answer here.

_____

_ _

_____

_____

_ _

_____

Laws are rules for communities. They help people live together. Laws are written down so everyone knows what they are. Laws help keep the community safe and clean. They help keep things fair.

Look at the pictures of the traffic lights. Find the red light. The red light tells drivers to stop. Stopping for a red light is one law you have in your community. This law helps keep the community safe for everyone.

 What does the green light tell car drivers? Write your answer here.

_____

- - - - - - - - - - - - - - - - - - - -

_____

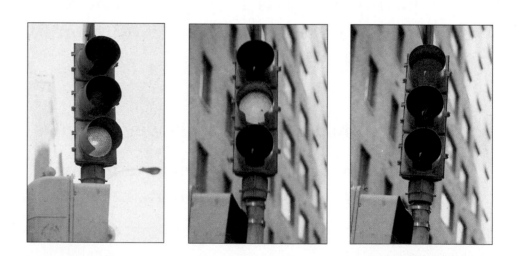

 Think about laws in your community. What is one law you must follow? Write your answer here.

_____

- - - - - - - - - - - - - - - - - - - -

_____

Match each law below with the correct picture. Write the number of the law in the box next to the picture.

1. Park in the street.

2. Walk your dog on a leash.

3. Throw litter in the litter basket.

Put a ✔ next to the picture that shows someone obeying the law.

UNIT
PROJECT
Tip

Think of a problem in your school. Talk with your team about this problem. How could the problem be fixed? Write down all your ideas.

Signs Help You

Signs tell you about rules and laws. The signs in your neighborhood help you remember the laws where you live. Some signs use words. Some signs just use pictures to help you remember rules or laws. Some signs even have lights to help you see them.

Look at these signs. Do you have them in your neighborhood? What do they tell you?

Your neighborhood and school have rules. Make a sign that shows one rule. Draw your sign here.

Read each question. Circle the correct answer.

1. Why do people make rules and laws?

Rules and laws cause problems.

Everyone likes rules and laws.

Rules and laws help people live together.

2. What rule is this girl breaking?

Do not make loud noises at night that may bother people.

Walk your dog on a leash.

Practice playing your horn every day.

3. Why does this neighborhood need a law about riding bicycles?

to keep children from having fun

to keep people safe

to keep things fair

 THINKING AND WRITING Name one rule or law you obeyed today. Tell how it helps people live together. Write your answer here.

_____

_____

_____

_____

Leaders and Laws

How are new laws made? How are old laws changed? Look at the picture below. These people are talking about a law in their community. They want to change the law.

The people talk to their community **leaders.** A leader is a person who leads or is in charge. Community leaders make up the **government.** The government is those people who make the laws and see that the laws are obeyed.

 What law would you like to change? Write your answer here.

70

Who are the community leaders? Communities have many leaders. Some communities have a **mayor.** The mayor is an important leader. The mayor works to keep the community a good place to live.

The people of a community choose their leaders. Each person gets to **vote** for, or pick, one person for each job. Then all the votes are counted. The person with the most votes is the leader.

Who is the leader of your community? What would you like to ask this person? Write your answer here.

_____

_____

_____

UNIT PROJECT Tip Talk to other children and adults in your school. Tell them your ideas for fixing the problem. Ask them If they have other ideas for fixing the problem. Make a list.

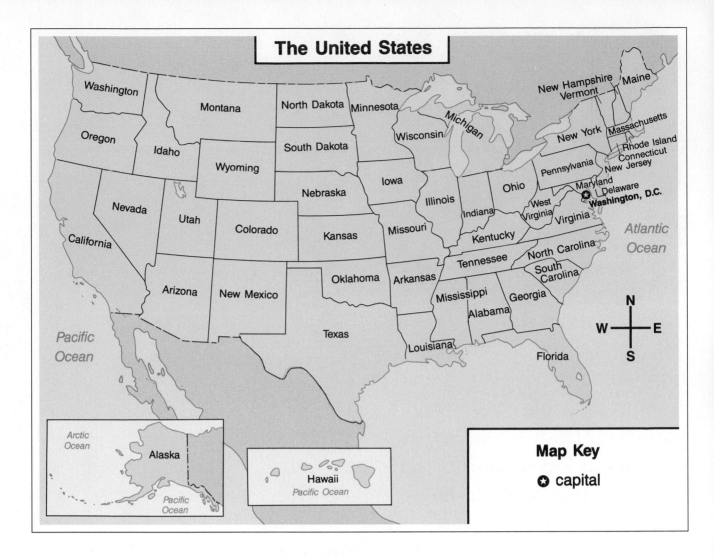

The United States

Map Key
⊗ capital

Your community is in a **state.** There are 50 states in the United States. Look at the map of the United States.

Look at the two boxes on the map that show Alaska and Hawaii. These are two of the states. They are far away from the other states. On maps of the United States, they are shown in boxes like these. These boxes are called **insets.**

 Look at the map of the United States. Find your state and circle the name.

Underline the names of the states that are next to your state.

Each state has a leader called the **governor.** The governor works to keep people in the state safe. The governor tries to make sure everyone is treated fairly.

The leader of the United States is the **President.** People in the United States vote to choose the President.

Government Leaders	
City or Town	Mayor
State	Governor
United States	President

 What is the name of your state's governor? Write your answer here.

_____

– – – – – – – – – – – – – – – – – – – –

_____

What is the name of the President of the United States? Write your answer here.

_____

– – – – – – – – – – – – – – – – – – – –

_____

Who leads your town? Is it a mayor? Write the name of your town's leader here.

_____

– – – – – – – – – – – – – – – – – – – –

_____

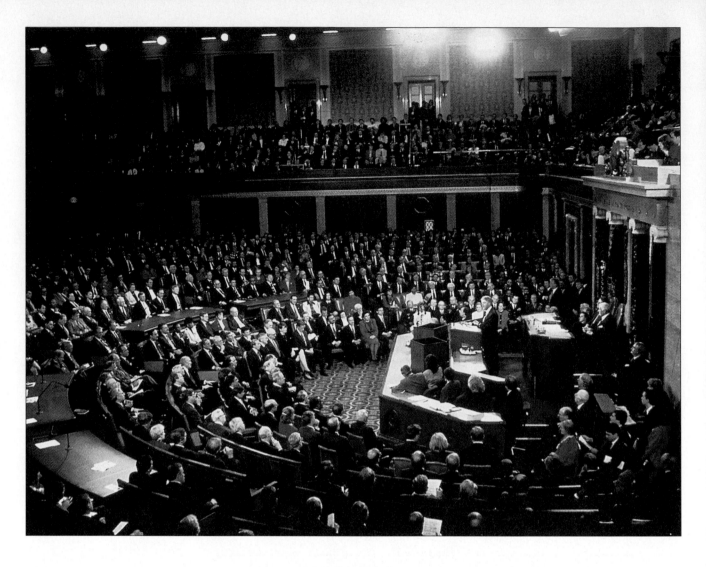

The **capital** is the city where the government meets. The governor and other state leaders work in the state capital.

The President works in the capital of the United States. The name of the capital of the United States is Washington, D.C. Leaders from all the states meet here. They make the laws for our country.

 What is the name of the capital of your state?

_____

_ _ _ _ _ _ _ _ _ _ _ _ _ _ _ _ _ _ _

_____

Long ago, much of the work on big farms was done by slaves. These slaves could not go to school or choose their jobs. The law said they were slaves. Frederick Douglass did not think this was fair. He spent his life working to change this law.

Frederick Douglass talked to President Lincoln about the slaves. He wrote in books and newspapers about the unfair law. Finally the law was changed. Slavery ended. Today, there are no slaves in the United States because Douglass helped get the law changed.

What can you do to change an unfair rule or law? How can you get it changed? Write your answer here.

_____

- -

_____

- -

_____

CHAPTER CHECKUP

Finish each sentence. Circle the correct answer.

1. People who make the rules for a community are the

teachers   leaders   children

2. People in a community choose their own leaders. Each person gets to

vote   rule   mayor

3. The leader of a state is the

mayor   President   governor

4. The leader of the United States is the

mayor   President   governor

Why is it important to have good leaders? Write your answer here.

_____

_____

_____

_____

_____

_____

CHAPTER 10

People Solve Problems Together

Sometimes people have a problem. They can try to fix it by working together.

Mr. Barker works at night. He sleeps during the day. After school, children play next to Mr. Barker's house. They make a lot of noise. The noise keeps Mr. Barker awake. He wants the children to stop playing near his house.

What can Mr. Barker do about the problem? Write your answer here.

_____

- - - - - - - - - - - - - - - - - - - -

_____

_____

- - - - - - - - - - - - - - - - - - - -

_____

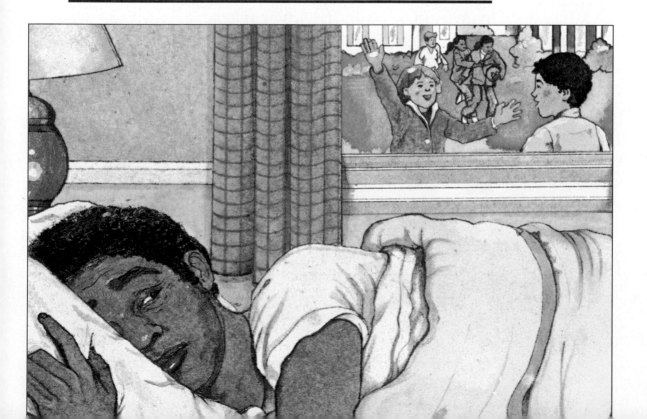

Mr. Barker talks with the children and their parents. The children do not have another place to play. What can they do?

Then they have an idea. There is a small field near Mr. Barker's house. No one uses the field. The grass is tall. Old cans, papers, and other trash are everywhere. The children and their parents and Mr. Barker talk. They decide to work together to clean up the field.

What needs to be done? Write your answer here.

On Mr. Barker's day off, everyone begins to work. It is hard work. It takes many days to finish the job. But now the children have a place to play. Mr. Barker can sleep.

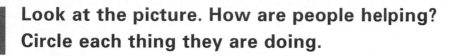 **Look at the picture. How are people helping? Circle each thing they are doing.**

digging

picking up cans and paper

washing the fence

raking the grass

The community leaders made the field into a community park. They put up signs where the children play. The signs remind people not to throw trash on the ground. Everyone helps keep the new park clean. It belongs to all of them.

Mr. Barker and his neighbors worked together to fix their problem. They also made their neighborhood a nicer place to live.

Think about your community. Can you make it a nicer place to live? Draw a picture of what you can do.

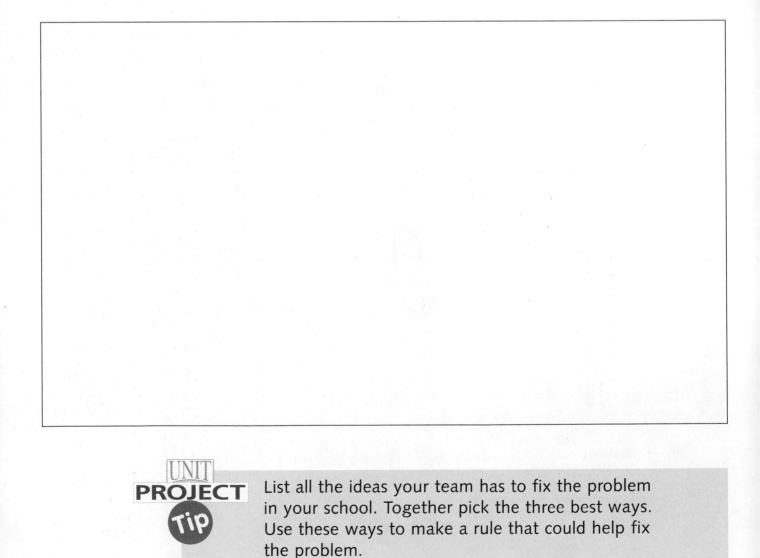

UNIT
PROJECT
Tip

List all the ideas your team has to fix the problem in your school. Together pick the three best ways. Use these ways to make a rule that could help fix the problem.

Mr. Barker and his neighbors worked to clean up a field. Sometimes cleaning up a community is a bigger job. The air, water, and land can get dirty. This is called **pollution.**

Pollution often covers a large area. Dirty air may blow from one state to another. A dirty river in your town may be dirty in other communities. These are big problems. Often, people in many communities must work together to clean up pollution.

Look at the picture. Pretend this place is in your community. How could your community make the air cleaner? Talk with your classmates about what you could do.

World Wildlife Fund

Sometimes people all around the world share a problem. They work together to fix it. One group that does this is the World Wildlife Fund. This group works to keep animals and the places they live safe.

The World Wildlife Fund is helping save tigers in Asia and elephants in Africa. It is working to save other animals around the world. The World Wildlife Fund is working to save rain forests and to keep the oceans clean.

 Make a poster for the World Wildlife Fund. Remind people to work together to protect our world and the animals living in it.

Tiger

Mountain Gorilla

Read each sentence. Write **T** on the line if the sentence is true. Write **F** if it is false.

_____ **1.** Problems can only be fixed by making new laws.

_____ **2.** People in a community can work together to fix their problems.

_____ **3.** Community leaders put up signs that tell us rules and laws.

_____ **4.** If the community cannot find an answer to a problem there is no one else to help.

 THINKING AND WRITING How could you stop people from throwing trash on the ground in your schoolyard? Think of two things you could do. Write your answers here.

_____

_____

_____

Reading a Map of the United States

Look at this map of the United States. Read each sentence. Do what it tells you to do.

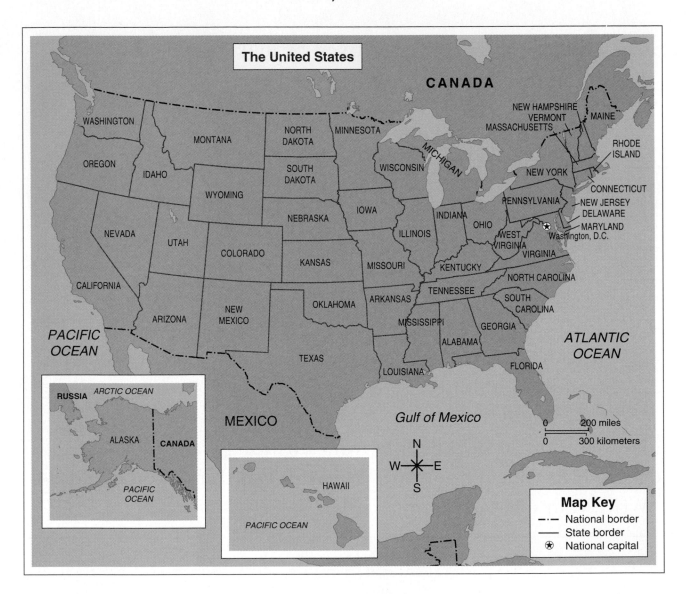

1. Circle the capital of the United States.

2. Color three states on the east coast red.

3. Color three states next to the Pacific Ocean blue.

4. Write an <u>N</u> on the north part of Alaska.

Now it's time to finish your project. Think about what you learned about problems that need to be fixed. Talk with your classmates. Answer these questions together.

- **What problems did you find in your school?**

- **What problems do other people think are important?**

- **What new rules could help fix the problems?**

Now decide how you will present your project. Try one of these ideas or one of your own ideas.

➤ Draw pictures to show what the problem is. Then make a new rule that could help fix the problem.

➤ Write a letter to your principal. Tell the principal about the problem. Then tell your team's idea for a new rule to fix the problem. Be sure everyone on your team helps write the letter. Everyone should sign his or her name to the letter.

➤ With your team act out the problem your team worked on. Then act out what things would be like if there was a rule that fixed the problem.

UNIT 5

Living Together in Neighborhoods

People in one neighborhood may have come from other cities, states, and countries around the world.

- How are these neighbors alike?
- How are they different?
- How do they share special times together?

UNIT PROJECT

Start a team project. Work with a group of classmates. Learn about special days people honor and how they honor them. Think about this as you read Unit 5.

Neighbors Are Alike and Different

Do you know where your neighbors are from? Many were born in the United States. Some came from other places in the world to live in your community.

Look at the picture of the people who live in this neighborhood. They all live in the United States now. Do they have the same color hair or skin? Are they the same age?

What is one way these neighbors are alike? What is one way these neighbors are different? Write your answers here.

_____

_ _ _ _ _ _ _ _ _ _ _ _ _ _ _ _ _ _

_____

_ _ _ _ _ _ _ _ _ _ _ _ _ _ _ _ _ _

_____

Carmen Sanchez

Look at the map below on pages 88 and 89. This is a map of the world. Can you find the United States on the map?

 Draw a green circle around the United States. Don't forget Alaska and Hawaii.

Carmen's family comes from Mexico. They speak Spanish and English at home. Her family cooks many foods from Mexico.

 Draw a line under the name of Mexico on the map.

Put a <u>C</u> on the continent that is south of Mexico.

Steven's grandparents came from Canada.

 Find Canada on the map. Draw a purple circle around it.

David's family comes from China. They speak Chinese. A special day for David's family is Chinese New Year.

 Find China on the map. Draw a blue circle around it.

What ocean is east of China? Write your answer here.

_____

- -

_____

Steven Smith

David Wong

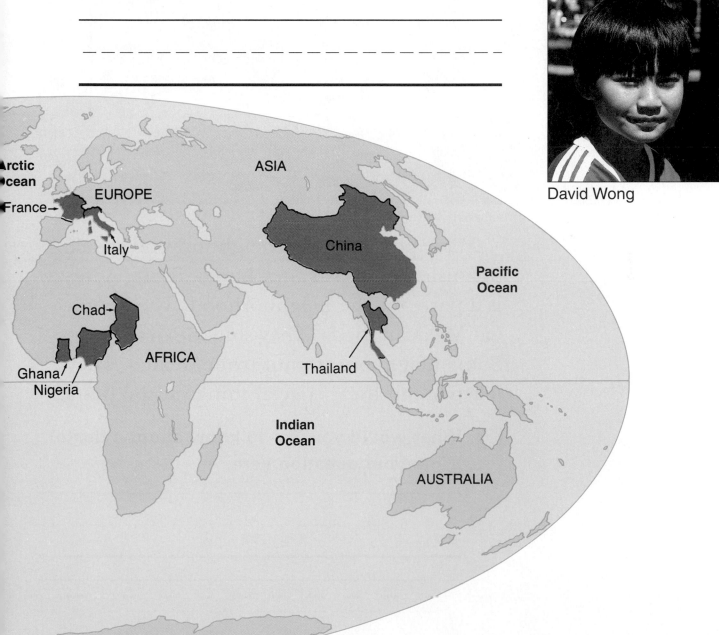

People from other countries help make the United States special. They bring their own ways of doing things. They fix many of the same foods here. They still enjoy special days. They share these special things with their new neighbors in the United States.

Many people in this neighborhood speak Spanish. Every year they have a fiesta. A fiesta is a party for the neighborhood. The people eat Mexican foods. They sing Mexican songs. Some neighbors are not from Mexico. They learn about these special things at the fiesta.

 What would you like to know about a fiesta? Write your question here.

_____

_____

_____

_____

Many people in this neighborhood are Chinese Americans. Look at the street signs. They are in English and in Chinese. So are some of the signs on stores.

How is this neighborhood like the one you live in? Write your answer here.

_____

_____

_____

_____

UNIT PROJECT Tip

Do you know any people from another country? Talk to them about their special days. Ask what they do on those days.

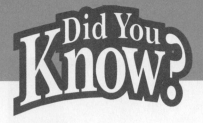

Becoming a Citizen

A **citizen** is a member of a country. People who move to the United States cannot be citizens right away. They must live here for a few years. They must learn to speak and read English. They must also learn about the United States.

After they have learned about the United States, then people can become citizens. They must promise to be good citizens. They must promise to follow the laws of the United States.

 What do you think a new citizen should know about the United States? Write your answer here.

_____

_____

_____

CHAPTER ✓ CHECKUP

Read each sentence. Find the word in the Word Box to finish each sentence. Write the word on the line.

Word Box

citizen
country
neighbors
world

1. People come to live in the United States from
_____

_ _ _ _ _ _ _ _ _ _ _ _ _ _ _ _ _

all over the _____ .

2. People bring their way of doing things when
_____

_ _ _ _ _ _ _ _ _ _ _ _ _ _ _ _ _ _ _ _

they move to a new _____ .

3. People from other countries share their special ways of doing
_____

_ _ _ _ _ _ _ _ _ _ _ _ _ _ _ _ _ _ _ _

things with their new _____ .

4. A member of a country is a
_____

_ _

_____ .

THINKING AND WRITING People from many countries live in the United States. How does this make our country better? Write your answer here.

_____

_ _

_____

_ _

_____

CHAPTER 12

Neighbors Celebrate Together

Have you ever watched a parade? What kind of parade was it? Many communities have a parade to **celebrate** a special day. To celebrate is to honor. People in a town come to watch or take part in the parade. Many communities have parades on the Fourth of July, Columbus Day, and St. Patrick's Day.

 Think about a parade you have seen. What did you like about it? Draw a picture here of the part you liked best.

 **PROJECT** **Tip** Talk with your classmates. Tell how your family celebrates a holiday. Do your classmates celebrate the holiday in the same way?

A **holiday** is a day to think about a special person or something special that happened. Holidays are celebrated in many ways. The Fourth of July celebrates the birthday of the United States. People celebrate this holiday by having picnics, parades, and fireworks with family and friends.

Why is it important to celebrate the Fourth of July? Write your answer here.

_____

_ _ _ _ _ _ _ _ _ _ _ _ _ _ _ _ _

_____

Look at the **time line** on these two pages. A time line shows a number of months or years in order. The marks on the time line stand for things that happened during those times. This time line shows the twelve months of the year. It shows when some of the holidays happen. The time line is like a picture of the year.

Which month comes after January? Write your answer here.

_____

- - - - - - - - - - - - - - - - - -

_____

Which month has two holidays? Write your answer here.

_____

- - - - - - - - - - - - - - - - - -

_____

New Year's Day

Martin Luther King Day

Memorial Day

Valentine's Day

January	February	March	April	May	June

Which holiday is in November? Write your answer here.

_____

- -

_____

Find Memorial Day on the time line. Circle it.

When is your birthday? Find the month. Add your birthday to the time line.

Think of one more holiday that your family celebrates. Add the holiday to the time line.

Fourth of July

Thanksgiving

July	August	September	October	November	December

Carmen Lomas Garza

Carmen Lomas Garza wanted to be an artist. As a little girl, she drew pictures of people, plants, and other things. Carmen went to school to learn to draw and paint. Today she is one of America's best artists.

Carmen Lomas Garza is also a writer. She has written a book about her family. She tells about her life as a little girl. She tells about her family celebrating special days. She painted the pictures for her book. All of the people in her pictures are people in her family or in her neighborhood.

 If you wrote about celebrating a special day, what day would it be?

_____

_ _

_____

People around the world celebrate holidays. They celebrate some of the same days you do. But people in other countries also celebrate in their own special ways.

New Year's Day is a holiday in the United States. We celebrate by having parties. We also have big parades. Children in Belgium write notes on paper they have decorated. The children read the notes to their families on New Year's Day. Many Chinese celebrate their New Year for four days.

Look at the pictures. How are these people celebrating their holidays? Write your answer here.

_____

_ _

_____

Read each sentence. Write **T** on the line if the sentence is true.
Write **F** if it is false.

_____ **1.** A holiday is a day to celebrate a person or something
special that happened.

_____ **2.** We celebrate all holidays the same way.

_____ **3.** On the Fourth of July, we celebrate the birthday of
the United States.

_____ **4.** You can use a time line to find out when things happen.

 Think about the holiday you like best. Why is it important to
celebrate this holiday? Write your answer here.

_____

_____

_____

_____

Unit 5 Skill Builder
Using a Time Line

Remember that a time line shows when things happen. This time line shows when some celebrations happen in different parts of the United States. Look at the time line. Then answer the questions.

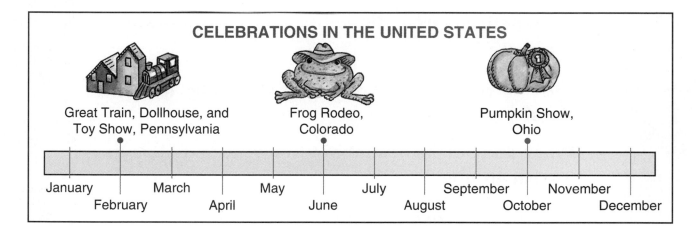

CELEBRATIONS IN THE UNITED STATES

Great Train, Dollhouse, and Toy Show, Pennsylvania

Frog Rodeo, Colorado

Pumpkin Show, Ohio

January   March   May   July   September   November
February   April   June   August   October   December

1. At what celebration would you see lots of pumpkins?

_____

_____

2. Where is the Great Train, Dollhouse, and Toy Show?

_____

_____

3. During what month is the Frog Rodeo?

_____

_____

Now it's time to finish your project. Think about what you learned about the holidays people in our country celebrate. Talk with your classmates about answers to these questions.

- **Do Americans from different countries celebrate the same holidays?**

- **How do your family and friends celebrate special days?**

- **What do you like best about the way the holidays are celebrated?**

Now decide how you will present your project. Use one of these ideas or one of your own ideas.

➤ Work with your team. Fix a part of your classroom to show how people celebrate holidays.

➤ Draw pictures to show how people celebrate. Put your team's drawings together in a booklet.

➤ Present a special news story to your class about how people celebrate in different ways. Have each member of your team tell about a different way of celebrating.

➤ Make a poster that tells people about a celebration that is coming soon. On your poster tell people the date of the celebration. Also tell how people will celebrate.

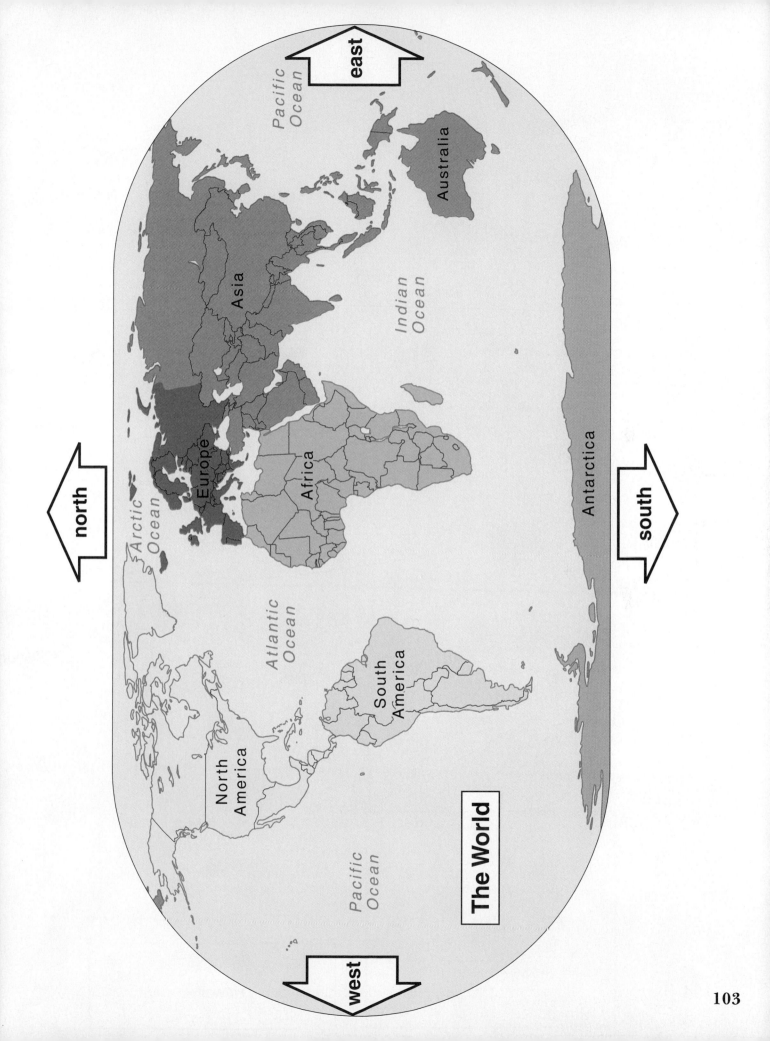

The World

north

south

east

west

Pacific Ocean

Arctic Ocean

Atlantic Ocean

Indian Ocean

Pacific Ocean

North America

South America

Europe

Africa

Asia

Australia

Antarctica

103

Washington

Oregon

Idaho

Montana

North Dakota

South Dakota

Wyoming

Nebraska

Nevada

Utah

Colorado

Kansas

west

California

Arizona

New Mexico

Oklahom

Texas

Alaska

Hawaii

104

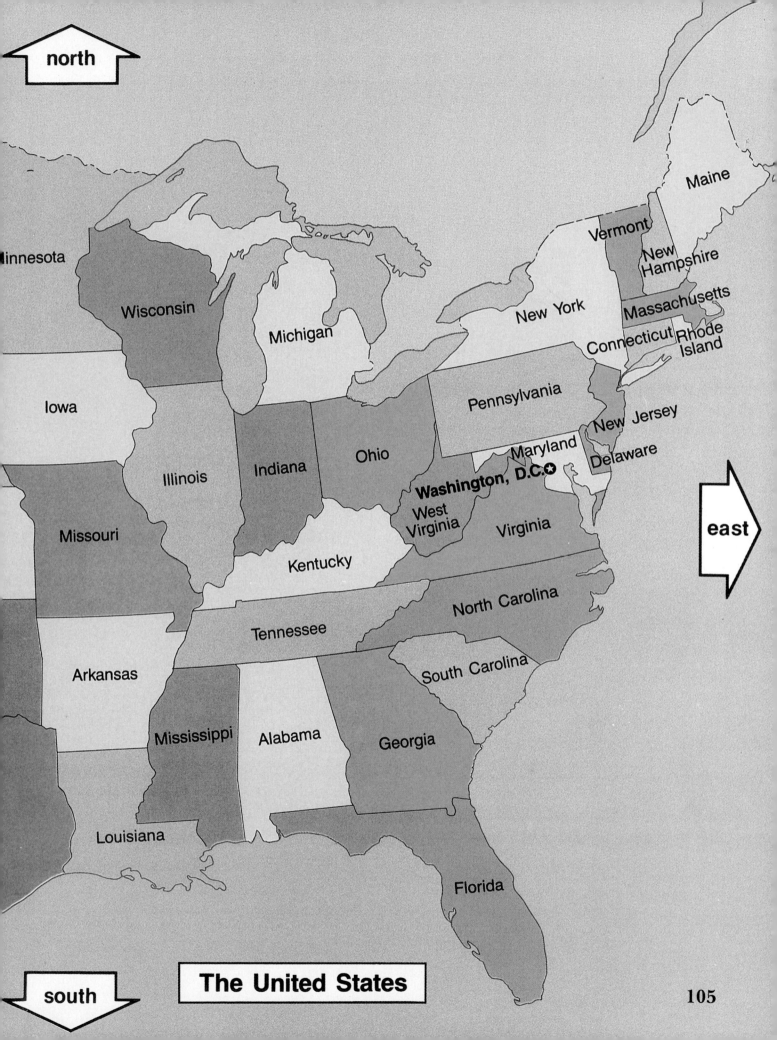

north

Minnesota

Wisconsin

Michigan

Maine

Vermont

New Hampshire

New York

Massachusetts

Connecticut

Rhode Island

Iowa

Pennsylvania

New Jersey

Illinois

Indiana

Ohio

Maryland

Delaware

Washington, D.C.⊙

Missouri

West Virginia

Virginia

east

Kentucky

Arkansas

Tennessee

North Carolina

South Carolina

Mississippi

Alabama

Georgia

Louisiana

Florida

The United States

south

105

Glossary

budget (page 54)
A budget is a plan for how to spend money.

buffalo (page 24)
Buffalo are large animals that lived on the plains. Some American Indians hunted buffalo.

buffalo

capital (page 74)
The capital is the city where the government meets. The governor works in the state capital.

celebrate (page 94)
To celebrate is to honor. You celebrate your birthday.

chart (page 26)
A chart puts facts in order.

citizen (page 92)
A citizen is a member of a country.

community (page 40)

A community is a town or city where people live, work, and play.

compass rose (page 9)

A compass rose helps you find directions on a map.

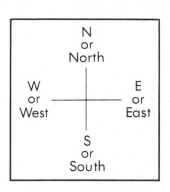

compass rose

continent (page 29)

A continent is a very large area of land. There are seven continents.

continent

directions (page 9)

The four directions are north, south, east, and west.

globe (page 30)

A globe is a model of Earth. It is round like a ball.

globe

goods (page 40)

Goods are things that people need and want. Some workers make goods for people to buy.

government (page 70)

The government is those people who make the laws and see that the laws are obeyed. The government is made up of community leaders.

governor (page 73)

The governor is the leader of a state.

holiday (page 95)

A holiday is a day to think about a special person or something special that happened. The Fourth of July is a holiday.

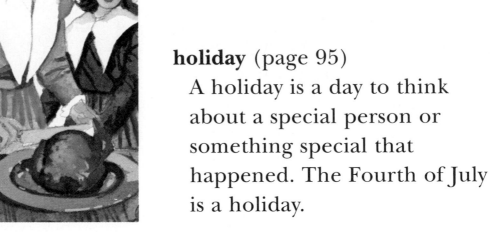

holiday

income (page 53)

Income is the money people get for doing a job. People use their income to buy the things they need and want.

inset (page 72)

An inset is a box on a map. An inset may show something that is too far away to be seen on the map.

invention (page 15)

An invention is something that is made for the first time.

law (page 66)

A law is a rule for a community, state, or country. Laws help keep things fair for everyone.

leader (page 70)

A leader is a person who leads or is in charge.

map (page 8)

A map is a drawing of a place.

map key (page 8)

A map key shows or tells what the pictures on a map mean.

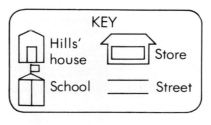

map key

mayor (page 71)

The mayor is an important leader of a community. The mayor helps make laws in a city or town.

mayor

mountain (page 10)

A mountain is very high land.

mountain

need (page 39)
A need is something a person must have to live. Food, clothes, and a place to live are needs that all people have.

neighbor (page 6)
A neighbor is someone who lives near you.

neighborhood

neighborhood (page 6)
A neighborhood is a place to live, work, and play.

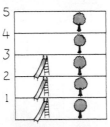
ocean

ocean (page 10)
An ocean is a very large body of salt water.

picture graph

picture graph (page 39)
A picture graph uses pictures to show facts.

plain (page 11)
A plain is land that is flat. It is a good place to farm.

plain

pollution (page 81)
Pollution is dirt, smoke, or trash. Pollution makes the air, water, and land dirty.

President (page 73)
   The President is the leader of
   the United States.

river (page 11)
   A river is a long stream of water
   that flows across land.

river

rule (page 64)
   A rule tells us what to do or
   what not to do.

savings (page 56)
   Savings is money that people
   keep for later.

service (page 42)
   A service is a job someone does
   to help other people.

service

slave (page 51)
   A slave is a person who is
   forced to work without pay.

state (page 72)
   There are 50 states in the
   United States. Each state is
   made up of many communities.

taxes (page 57)

Taxes is money people pay to the community where they live. Taxes help pay for things like building roads and schools.

time line

born	measles	school
1980	1983	1986

time line (page 96)

A time line shows things that happened during a certain amount of time.

volunteer (page 51)

A volunteer is a person who chooses to work without pay.

vote (page 71)

A vote is a choice. People of a community vote for their leaders. Each person gets to pick one person for each job.

wants

want (page 39)

A want is something a person would like to have but can live without. Toys, trips, and pets are things that some people would like to have.